A Spot to Haunt

Level 4+
Blue+

Helpful Hints for Reading at Home

The graphemes (written letters) and phonemes (units of sound) used throughout this series are aligned with Letters and Sounds. This offers a consistent approach to learning, whether reading at home or in the classroom.

THIS BLUE+ BOOK BAND SERVES AS AN INTRODUCTION TO PHASE 5. EACH BOOK IN THIS BAND USES ALL PHONEMES LEARNED UP TO PHASE 4, WHILE INTRODUCING ONE PHASE 5 PHONEME. HERE IS A LIST OF PHONEMES FOR THIS PHASE, WITH THE NEW PHASE 5 PHONEME. AN EXAMPLE OF THE PRONUNCIATION CAN BE FOUND IN BRACKETS.

Phase 3			
j (jug)	v (van)	w (wet)	x (fox)
y (yellow)	z (zoo)	zz (buzz)	qu (quick)
ch (chip)	sh (shop)	th (thin/then)	ng (ring)
ai (rain)	ee (feet)	igh (night)	oa (boat)
oo (boot/look)	ar (farm)	or (for)	ur (hurt)
ow (cow)	oi (coin)	ear (dear)	air (fair)
ure (sure)	er (corner)		

New Phase 5 Phoneme	au (haunt, haul, taunt)

HERE ARE SOME WORDS WHICH YOUR CHILD MAY FIND TRICKY.

Phase 4 Tricky Words			
said	were	have	there
like	little	so	one
do	when	some	out
come	what		

TOP TIPS FOR HELPING YOUR CHILD TO READ:

- Allow children time to break down unfamiliar words into units of sound and then encourage children to string these sounds together to create the word.

- Encourage your child to point out any focus phonics when they are used.

- Read through the book more than once to grow confidence.

- Ask simple questions about the text to assess understanding.

- Encourage children to use illustrations as prompts.

This book introduces the phoneme /au/ and is a Blue+ Level 4+ book band.

A Spot to Haunt

Written by
Robin Twiddy

Illustrated by
Danielle Webster-Jones

This is Saul, and Saul is a spook. His job is to haunt.

Saul has been haunting this spot for years and years. Until this night.

Now Saul is looking for a better spot to haunt. What is a spook with no haunt?

He is looking for a fresh spot to haunt. Can he get one on the internet?

A pond. Saul has never been to a pond. Can Saul haunt a pond?

Saul thinks the pond will be a good spot. He starts to haunt the ducks.

But ducks do not fear things that drop from trees.

The pond is no good. Saul is off to look for a better spot to haunt.

Is this a good spot to haunt, Saul?
There are desks and lamps.

Saul flicks the lights on and off. Will this spook them?

"It is just the power," tuts the boss.
There is no fear in this room.

No, this is not a good spot to haunt.
Saul floats off.

Saul sees a crowd. They will be fun to haunt, he thinks.

One of them is hauling bricks. Saul thinks he can get him to drop the bricks.

Saul has a plan. With a tug, the man's pants can be seen.

The crowd taunt him.
"Oi, Paul, get a belt!" they holler.

Still, no one is afraid. Saul looks for a better spot to haunt.

Saul needs to get a good spot to haunt soon. Will this rocket launch do?

Saul gets into the cockpit and starts to go, "Woo-oo-oo-oo."

No one can hear Saul. They have helmets! 3... 2... 1... The rocket is off.

This is no good. There must be a spot for Saul to haunt.

Saul floats from street to street. A spook with no haunt is no spook at all.

This is a bit of town that he has never been to.

Saul feels good floating under the moon, next to the trees and flowers.

Boo! A spook winks and hugs Saul.
Saul sees that spooks fill the yard.

This is not just a spot to haunt, he thinks. Saul feels that he belongs.

A Spot to Haunt

1) Why does Saul need to look for a spot to haunt?

2) How does Saul try to spook the first group of people?

   a) Playing the drums
   b) Turning lights on and off
   c) Cooking a lovely dinner

3) Where does Saul feel like he belongs?

4) Would you be scared of Saul? Why or why not?

5) How would you make someone afraid if you were Saul?

© This edition published in 2023. First published in 2022.
BookLife Publishing Ltd.
King's Lynn, Norfolk, PE30 4LS, UK

ISBN 978-1-80155-169-4

All rights reserved. Printed in Poland.
A catalogue record for this book is available from the British Library.

A Spot to Haunt
Written by Robin Twiddy
Illustrated by Danielle Webster-Jones

An Introduction to BookLife Readers...

Our Readers have been specifically created in line with the London Institute of Education's approach to book banding and are phonetically decodable and ordered to support each phase of the Letters and Sounds document.

Each book has been created to provide the best possible reading and learning experience. Our aim is to share our love of books with children, providing both emerging readers and prolific page-turners with beautiful books that are guaranteed to provoke interest and learning, regardless of ability.

BOOK BAND GRADED using the Institute of Education's approach to levelling.

PHONETICALLY DECODABLE supporting each phase of Letters and Sounds.

EXERCISES AND QUESTIONS to offer reinforcement and to ascertain comprehension.

BEAUTIFULLY ILLUSTRATED to inspire and provoke engagement, providing a variety of styles for the reader to enjoy whilst reading through the series.

AUTHOR INSIGHT:
ROBIN TWIDDY

Robin Twiddy is one of BookLife Publishing's most creative and prolific editorial talents, who imbues all his copy with a sense of adventure and energy. Robin's Cambridge-based first class honours degree in psychosocial studies offers a unique viewpoint on factual information and allows him to relay information in a manner that readers of any age are guaranteed to retain. He also holds a certificate in Teaching in the Lifelong Sector, and a postgraduate certificate in Consumer Psychology.

A father of two, Robin has written over 70 titles for BookLife and specialises in conceptual, role-playing narratives which promote interaction with the reader and inspire even the most reluctant of readers to fully engage with his books.

This book introduces the phoneme /au/ and is a Blue+ Level 4+ book band.